MY NANA'S HANDS

POEMS

MY NANA'S HANDS

POEMS

Elodia Esperanza Benitez

RIOT OF ROSES
PUBLISHING HOUSE
SEJATNGA
UNCEDED TONGVA TERRITORY
SOUTH WHITTIER, CALIFORNIA

Praise for *My Nana's Hands*

Elodia Esperanza Benitez's poetry collection, My Nana's Hands sings with the music of her neighborhood, because it is the music of her heart. We are held by her loving and powerful Nana's hands, guided by her strength and her wisdom. We get to taste sopa de Estrella, and salivate over delicious tamales and chisme. We get to hang out with the tías, tíos and primas at family parties. There are also moments of quiet reflection and longing, moms that have to work a lot, brothers that get caught up in an unjust system, absent fathers, and violent men. We see the sights unique to the central valley, the farmworkers, the people on the bus Number 68. All told with the sharp eyes of a poeta who understands her community and brings them to page as a "sentinel of memory", to spread "semillas we leave behind, water them to grow for tomorrows garden". We remember the garden, we remember the women, we remember their sacrifice and love. It's a powerful chorus of women that shout from the page. I hear them, I hear them in my bones, that is the power of being your own hero, of being "re-conquistadoras, takers of what you said they can't have". These poems transport you in time and place. Isn't that what we do? We bend time and space to tell our stories. You will feel the oldies and the drums beat. What a bendición to read these words!

-Jesenia Chavez, Author of This Poem Might Save You (Me)

Elodia Benitez's poetry is so vivid and descriptive, it takes me back to the days when I laid in bed and pinched my own grandmother's hands, hands that were also "like cinnamon freckled pillows." I can hear and feel and smell the hustle and bustle of crowded houses where families gather, children play, and ordinary Mexican dishes come to life, transforming a simple sopa de letras into a "sea of stars." All of these poems are "planted memories," memories which Elodia's Nana planted deep within the author herself, memories that Elodia lovingly harvests, bringing to the table colores y sabores that we can all cherish.

-Diosa Xochiquetzalcóatl, Author of West of the Santa Ana and Other Sacred Places

Elodia Benitez's memoir-in-verse takes the reader down emotional avenue after emotional highway. Benitez has the reader travel from San Ysidro to Gilroy, among other areas, as they appear, back-in-time. Nana Julia is luminous all around, whether she is making tamales or planting roses of wisdom for her kin. With that saying, "Never let a poet lie to you," in mind, it is clear the narrator is not lying to us about someone who is truly selfless. Nana is alive in verse for her families, family friends, and readers' future generations.

-Jesse Tovar, Editor, Lit Stack, litstack.substack.com

Published by Riot of Roses Publishing House

My Nana's Hands

Copyright © 2023, Elodia Esperanza Benitez
ISBN: 978-1-961717-08-4
ISBN: 978-1-961717-07-7
Library of Congress Control Number: 2023921058

Cover Art
©Armando Franco, 2023

First Edition, 2023

To request permissions, you may contact the Publisher at riotofrosesllc@gmail.com
Printed in the United States of America.

www.riotofrosespublishinghouse.com

Cover design by www.arrowupz.com
Layout design by www.arrowupz.com
Edited by Brenda Vaca

These poems are dedicated to my Nana,
Julia Barrientos Benitez,
who loved me into all that I am.
And to my grandmother,
Elodia Romero Villa,
who left behind a name and a legacy of love.

CONTENTS

FOREWORD

I met Elodia Esperanza Benitez long before she remembers having crossed paths with me. She was somewhere around the age of twelve, navigating middle school, busy noticing the world around her. I imagine her documenting her reality in a journal at that age, keeping our existence safe in the *tinta sagrada* of pages she has tended to over the years. I knew little of her at the time, other than what little I could observe in my role as an adult, and still it was enough to know she was surrounded by strong *mujeres* who had planted seeds of their hopes and dreams into the legacy of who she was born to be.

Flash forward to crossing paths again, years later, and she is co-facilitating a youth program for young women, grounding them in the power of culture beyond resilience. She is at that writer's crossroads, coming into that space most writers *de corazón* who write to right against our erasure come to, that space of inevitability, where the writings eventually obligate us to bring them out of the shadows, and by extension, bring ourselves into the light.

It is now years later, and we've survived a pandemic, *comadreado movidas* in backyard patios, marched alongside each other with fists up in the air, spoken fire into microphones, held audiences in collective *apapachos*, and reminded folks to take that *suspiro de alivio*. I witnessed her go for it, *a la brava*, as she published her first chapbook *Love in Many Faces*, and I have had the privilege of seeing our shared communities beam with pride.

Through this collection, so fittingly named *My Nana's Hands,* Elodia Esperanza Benitez has a way of seeing us, all of us, fully human, beyond aspirational narratives, and completely in our dignity. In resistance against the insistence of keeping us unnamed, invisible, and in the shadows, she offers us a symphony of names in declaration of our humanity. The collection reads like a living time capsule of sorts, one that is both timeless and unburied, as she offers glimpses into our shared *recuerdos* of sitting in family living rooms overhearing recipes of survival, sitting on our front steps soothed by the soundtrack of our neighborhoods, and of overhearing the background banter during *comadre* phone calls of the real-life novelas of all our *chismes.* The poems center *gente* and defy the external gaze that has wielded the weight of shame to withhold love from our communities. She does this simply and powerfully throughout. For instance, how freshly cleaned Corteses become regalia; how she weaves the lyrics of *Un Dia a La Vez* into "The Ballad of Imelda Alejo Villa" and revisits the ballad in parts throughout, weaving across generations to put names to faces as she calls on us to bear witness to the implications; how she vividly documents our cruising of the neighborhood while weaving together a constellation of *gente* and our stories, whether we are cruising the streets in lowriders or on foot; and how she guides the reader through a slow cruise of the songs and sounds of our neighborhood, by including both the bitter and the sweet of our memories. Through the pages held here, Nana lives forever, along with all of our grandmothers, *las abuelitas,* defying stereotypes of Mama Coco tropes, who while nostalgic and relatable, flatten the reality of our stories. Like Nana's hands, the poems feel like a tender *apapacho,* wiping tears from our cheeks, reminding us we matter, looking us right in the eyes, reminding us we are seen and we are loved. In Nana's hands, we are *masa,* nourishing sustenance, guided by her hand as we reveal our own shape in honor of the legacy she has co-created. As the poet Elodia Esperanza Benitez affirms in her closing poem "We Sit Graveside" when she leaves us with:

"Nanas live forever in the love and words they plant within us."

In Nana's hands, we are nurtured whole even with the browning imperfection of our leaves, tended to, seen, con cariño and a dash of tough love. Through Elodia's words, Nana lives forever.

C/S

Rosanna Alvarez, 2023 International Latino Book Awards Award Winning Author of *Braided [Un]Be-Longing, Ocote Libre Press*

MY NANA'S HANDS

My Nana's hands are
like cinnamon freckled pillows,
plump and cool against my cheek.
My favorite thing is
to hold them in my small hands,
to measure the length of our fingers.
Hers are so long with
their jeweled claws.
I wonder how
she grew them so long.
They're good for
scratching scalps free from tight trenzas,
picking out my moquitos,
and for stirring Sweet n' Low into her coffee.
They're best for
wiping my face and
pulling me soft to her pigeon chest.
My favorite thing is
to hold my Nana's hands in mine,
read her palms,
and tell her she's going to live forever.

SAN YSIDRO PARK

Airwalks with frayed laces,
hair pulled tight stiff,
baby hairs slicked down,
my prima Diana's old dress
her mom says
she can't wear 'cause she's too gorda.
Flying down sidewalks
on ankle bite scooters
past practicing danzantes,
homies playing handball,
Saturday birthday parties,
call of the drum giving tempo
to oldies playing smooth out of portable speakers.
Climbing up carved slides,
reading graffiti calling cards
that decorate playgrounds,
twisting swing chains until the world spins,
my cousin's laugh,
    rubber beat bounce off concrete walls,
                pounding drums,
paletero horns,
and back around to my cousin
who says it's her turn.

No, her mom who is my tia,
but really my cousin three times removed says,
Ya `sta la comida.
I pretend I can't hear.
She doesn't like me anyways,
says I'm traviesa,
don't listen,
and no, you can't spend the night.
I wind the chain,
and watch my world spin.

SAVANNAH'S SEVENTH BIRTHDAY

Go to Walmart to buy Powerpuff Girl decorations,
the 99 cent store for the plates, napkins, and everything else.
Head over to Del Sol for the piñata and to order the jumper.
Tell Chana to bring some waters and juices.
Tell Ruben to bring his extra cooler for the beers.
Who is making the rice?
Put the beans to cook in the crockpot overnight, no hassle.
Chips, salsa, ketchup, mustard, an onion to clean the grill,
head to the park early to save a spot and set up.
Ask Veronica to bring her car so she can load up the food.
Buy the meat, buy the ice, buy a new white shirt for Carlos.
Remember to bring the chairs, remember to bring the speaker.
Remember to tell Lisa the party starts at 12,
so she'll be on time at 2.
What? They're already there with the jumper?
Hang on….

JASMINE'S FACE

Jasmine Barrientos
has her mother's oval face,
her Nana's straight figure,
her Big Nana's
big curly hair.
Doesn't look much
like the dad
who named her,
named and left
in the same breath.
Can't see
him in herself.
She glimpses him
behind peeked doors
with clothes hanging,
with backpack hanging,
red-brown face hanging,
tweaker's noose.
Nothing for her?
No food stamps
to buy your daughter
some cereal?
No money for school?
You like these streets?
Jasmine's mom asks.

Get your act together son,
Nana says.
Not for himself,
not for his daughter,
all he can give
is a name.
Good.
In this way
she is made
of only women.
Tweakers take:
money, bikes, phones,
expectations.
They can't give faces.

MI TÍA PILA PALOMA

Mi Tía Pila Paloma,
whose apartment smells like
moth balls and musty dresses
and Avon lotions.
That's how she likes it.
And don't be so ornery.
God doesn't like it.
Don't be so selfish,
because God can see you.
And *Por favor mija,*
don't ever let a boy touch you down there.
This from mi Tía Pila Paloma.
And when I tell my Nana
she scowls.
Says it's cause Tía had the white owl put on her,
running around with Danny Sanchez,
who didn't come back from the war.
You remember Danny Sanchez, right?
Ay, I thought he was so handsome.
He used to drive that beautiful Chevy.
I saw his sister at bingo the other night.
That new medication has her looking so skinny.
Whatever happened to his wife, Crazy Carmen?
That old witch?
Think she moved to Los Baños with her daughter.

Later, sitting on top of paper piles,
mi Tía Pila Paloma points to a photo.
See her.
She says about a sepia beauty with her blouse pulled low,
eyes bright,
mouth pulled up fresh.
Someone should have told her.

SOPA DE ESTRELLAS

Lilia measures time in the years
before she could reach her Nana's stove.
And the years after,
when she was big enough to stir the sopa.
Lilia loves
when her Nana makes sopa de estrellas,
a sea of stars she blows apart,
bringing up brow sweat on hot summer days,
her elbows sticking to thick plastic table covers,
her favorite.
Sopitas measure the years,
this she knows.
Same as she knows without looking
how much chicken bouillon to add.
Sopita de coditos for little babies with new teeth,
sopa de conchas for kids
running in from outside
with dirty hands and hair all jacked up,
sopa de fideo,
respectable and served with tortillas
for visiting tios
sighing into glasses of water
when they'd rather be drinking Coke.
Still, sopa de estrellas are just for her.

SITTING OUTSIDE THE PROBATION OFFICE

Sitting outside the probation office,
leather sticking to the back of my legs,
sun on my left arm,
brother by my right arm,
waiting on my dad to come out,
big bottle of water and a pack of sunflower seeds
sitting in the cup holder
of my dad's Cutlass Supreme.
I'm sitting outside of the probation office
munching on Hot Cheetos,
sipping on an Arizona tea,
and watching men in long shorts
and Ecko shirts walk up.
I've got my book to read,
but I'm playing "I Spy" with my brother
to keep him from getting bored.
I spy with my little eye…
A pitbull in the backseat of a Yukon,
windows cracked for him,
just like us.
If anyone asks,
he probably has to say he's twelve too.

ON POLK CT.

Christmas Eve '02

I am the only girl in a herd of boy cousins and brothers.
They crowd into Lil Gilbert's room
that used to be Big Gilbert's room.
The room I share with my little brother Anthony
used to be our dad's room too.
Anthony is named after dad too,
but we call him by his middle name.
My hair is moussed and gelled into a hard shell on top,
no amount of tapping on my head will loosen it.
All I get is Mama slapping my hand down for good measure.
My shiny black shoes are creased from running around,
the polyester lace of my Christmas dress itches.
Nana's house is packed with Tías and Tíos;
Tía Norma brings the diet sodas and scolds me more
when her grandkids are visiting from San Diego.
They are the ones I never see.
Aunt Veronica got married and moved herself far away.
She's got a nice house in the Valley somewhere.
My Nino just came home from The War,
very tall and very brown.
I stumble through the saludos.
My own dad isn't tall when
he stops by to ask Nana for a few dollars.

He eats a plate without looking at me once.
Tío Hector is watching an old Western on the TV.
Cousin Rachel is loud and red faced.
I hear Tía Norma telling Nana *she better not start.*
Food is packed on the kitchen table.
Rachel made the beans and macaroni salad.
Mama made the rice this year.
Nana's been steaming tamales for days on her rattling stove.
The tree sits in the corner,
burgundy and gold 'cause Mama decorated it this year.
Mama wears burgundy lip liner,
she looks very pretty in her cream sweater.
Presents piled all around,
mostly for my cousins who bring them in big black bags.
I'm hoping for a Barbie with copper brown hair to match mine.
I won't know until midnight.

BIG NANA'S APARTMENT

Ruby knows the rules
when she visits her Big Nana's apartment.
She does this once a week with her Mama
to take Tata to run errands,
and dust the high shelves and mop the floors.
She has to wipe her feet,
it's very clean inside.
It smells of the powder soap
Tata washes the curtains in.
Everything in its place:
photos of pastel Jesus in foiled gold,
black-and-whites of dark haired men
in front of old trucks.
Couches are laid over with a crocheted throw.
Ruby kisses Big Nana and Tata on the cheek.
Their cheeks are wonderfully soft,
thin-skinned and lined.
There is no running, no yelling,
no wiggling in Big Nana's apartment.
The TV is always playing *Caso Cerrado*.
There is a room ready and plain
for when Uncle Ernesto gets out of prison.
Ruby has never met Uncle Ernesto.
Big Nana likes to talk.
Tata doesn't talk much at all.

Ruby sits still to hear Big Nana tell stories.
Always the same three;
when she left school to work at thirteen,
when she met her first husband,
when her second husband put hands on her,
and she threw him out.
Ruby listens like it's the first time she's heard it.
Mama finishes the floors,
asks Tata if he's ready to go.
Ruby gives Big Nana another kiss,
she waves it off with a scoff.

ESTHER MAGDALENA

Esther Magdalena
baptized in a puff of white taffeta
in her sixth week of life
by her mother's favorite prima
and her father's brother,
who goes from Tío to Nino,
announces at her cousin Santi's birthday
that she will never marry.
This way
she can leave parties whenever she wants.
She dyes her black brown hair
blue black.
Wants to fight Lizbeth from school,
that bitch knows why.
Pierces her own lip,
bites at the scar it leaves,
plays Morrissey loud in her brother's truck,
lets her boyfriend give her a hand tattoo,
breaks that hand landing a trick wrong.
Some evenings it's all her mother can do,
to sigh into her café and ask,
"What am I going to do with that girl?"

PLANTED PALM TREE

The sun rises East
bringing up people who make the day
by toil of soil
laid claim to by others.
My Mother came up to plant a palm tree in my Nana's yard,
kissed each open hand leaf,
and left to tend other gardens.
Nana brought out her plastic chair
to hold vigil with the little palm,
green cut garden hose spouting out gentle admonitions
to us children playing in its wake.
Nana spoke life to will the tree grow.
And we all paused to sit curbside,
dyeing our teeth with raspberry raspados,
eyes trained on her in all her flowered apron glory,
willing her to stay.
The sun descended West,
laying people to rest.
Nana stood with a sermon sigh,
"The palm was brought here,
planted without ceremony
and will still grow tall enough to greet the sun
now that I've watered the roots."

DELIVERING TAMALES

Nine,
and the world is as big as Nana's Oldsmobile can travel.
She keeps her burned CD Spanish ballads
in a zipped up album under the seat,
blue plastic rosary dancing
from where it dangles on the rearview mirror.
The belt presses against my neck,
hot because we're driving West,
hot on the cloth seats,
foil wrapped bundles next to me.
My favorite street in Gilroy is lined with trees,
and shade where the sun peeks through in spots.
Each house a different kind of pretty,
but all the driveways are clean and uncracked.
Having money means a clean driveway
with the perfect slope to scooter down.
No broken concrete or oil stains to get caught up in.
The backseat smells of pork and masa.
My hands smell of masa.
My hair is steamed in it.
My Nana makes the best tamales,
lots of orders to deliver.
We pull up and I rush out to deliver,
collect Nana's money.

It's mostly school secretaries from Tía Gloria's school.
They give Tía their orders.
School secretaries love their tamales
and their nice driveways.
We finish
and Nana turns the Oldsmobile
back East towards home.
The sun's warmth is cooling from our backs.

TWELVE

Nothing is right at twelve.
Hips came in too soon.
Tía's husband keeps staring.
Mami came in too late...again.
Baby brother is hungry.
Asks, *"What's for dinner?"*
Sopita made with ketchup.
Haven't seen Andres since they locked him away.
Haven't seen dear old dad in months.
Thank God.
Esperanza, if y=mx+b,
how long until pg&e shuts off the lights?
Algebra teacher asks to make sense of letters in numbers.
Can hardly make sense of life.
Twelve,
nothing is right at twelve.
But nobody bothers to ask
a little girl with too much attitude
why she spits.
Nobody except —
another twelve year old girl
caked up in Maybelline face powder
and thick winged liner
she stole from Walgreens.

She hates her brother's girlfriend,
fought her in the sala over the weekend.
She wishes she could hate her dad.
"Ey, you wanna see this guy I'm talking to?
He's hella annoying but I was bored."
Twelve,
nothing is right at twelve.
Sometimes they laugh until they cry,
mascara running.
Dream away traumas.
Borrow their parent's music.
Make it their own.
"Damn dude, that sucks
Do you want to spend the night at my house?
We can play comadres and drink coffee."
Twelve,
nothing is ever right at twelve,
except other twelve-year-old girls.

MY PRIMA DANIELA'S WEDDING

My prima Daniela's wedding,
wedding down in San Ysidro,
Down South,
down South, far enough to see over into Tijuana,
into Tijuana, where my Grandpa has a little house,
little house stuck into the hillside,
hillside cemeteries, where they buried my Tio Rogelio,
my Tio Rogelio, with his vices and pain,
pain of loss, a Mama's loss,
loss that followed her sons and daughters,
daughters like my own Mama,
my own Mama never knew much about being a Mama,
a Mama who worked hard and pulled braids,
braids she put in my hair, tight with ribbons,
purple colored ribbons for my prima Daniela's wedding.

THE BALLAD OF IMELDA ALEJO
VILLA: PART ONE

Un día a la vez, Dios mío
Suffer the little children,
bring them to their mother.
But she was shot down,
taken by the jealousy
of another.

Es lo que pido de ti
Imelda Alejo Villa,
beautiful in the old way,
in a bold way,
in the calluses of her hands,
never knew a man
she feared.

Dame la fuerza para vivir
This bravery,
she combed
into her sons' and daughter's hair.
Weaving prayers into strands
through her mother's hands
to last a lifetime.

Un dia a la vez
The neighbors all warned,
this man, this faceless man,
if he can't have you…
Imelda scorned,
she belonged to
no man,
as evidenced by the calluses,
on her beautiful hands.

LA BALADA DE IMELDA ALEJO
VILLA: PRIMERA PARTE

Un día a la vez, Dios mío
Dejen que los niños vengan.
Llévalos a su madre,
pero ella fue derribada.
Tomado por los celos
    de otro.

Es lo que pido de ti
Imelda Alejo Villa,
hermosa al estilo antigua,
de una manera valiente,
con los callos de sus manos,
nunca conoció a un hombre
que ella temía.

Dame la fuerza para vivir
Esta valentía ella peinó
en el cabello de sus hijos e hijas.
Tejiendo oraciones en trenzas
a través de las manos de su madre
para durar toda la vida.

Un día a la vez
Todos los vecinos advirtieron
que este hombre, este hombre sin rostro.
Si él no puede tenerte...
Imelda con desprecia juró
ella pertenecía a
ningún hombre.
Como es evidente con los callos
de sus manos hermosas.

LOS XV AÑOS DE ANGELA LOPEZ

Neveah Lopez and her family
don't travel for reasons not borne of invitations,
arching Spanish under hot glued ribbon.
Quinces, Bautismos, Funerales,
the Holy Trinity of Mexican parties.
This trip down South to Perris for
"Los XV Años de Angela Lopez."
Neveah sleeps wrapped up in her blanket,
her mom blasting Los Cadetes de Linares the whole way.
She's got years of sleeping through noise.
Little prima Angela wanted a rose gold dress,
a surprise dance to a Peso Pluma song,
enchilada plates with warm caesar salad,
a rose gold dress with plastic lined dirt on the bottom,
a princess with a court of girls in Converse,
chambelanes with dark pomade hair.
They have their father's name,
but their mother's face.
A parade of horses on dancing feet,
older tías and tíos dancing cumbias better than the young folk,
a DJ telling everyone when to applaud,
announcing the *Caballo Dorado.*

Proud parents in their, *"Gracias a todos por venir…"*
Neveah watches the Quinceñera,
watches her duck down shy when it's her turn to speak.
These trips, these Holy Trinity trips…

ITZEL, SACRED GIRL

Itzel, sacred girl,
whose hair braided thick,
wore colorful ribbons cascading down her back.
One day,
tired of passersby tugging at them,
she took a knife,
and hacked them off.
Let the ribbons fall where they may.

A LIFE THROUGH HOLES IN THE WALL

Marlen can tell stories by the holes in the walls of her home.
Where she pulled out the ironing board without looking,
the heel dent from playing WWE with her cousins,
the hole covered up by the couch from moving it,
to build a living room fort.
Marlen knows:
the holes from fights,
the "Dad Can't Keep a Job" Fight,
the "Mom Doesn't Want to Go to the Party" Fight,
the "Cheating Texts" Fight,
the "Pack Your Shit" Fight.
Marlen knows the holes stay as reminders.
Next time…
She takes her fist,
holds it up to see if it fits.

LITTLE PRIMAS

They start out small. Our little primas. Silver teeth traviesas, hair pulled tight into sock buns. Who eat our chips, use our phones to play games, scream every time the jump house gets knocked over. Hummingbirds who fly through parties with glee, fluttering only seconds to eat half a taco. Who watch us curl our hair with studied concentration. Easy to love. When they call to see if you're coming to the party. Huitzilin. Go for rides to the store with us. Go pick one thing only. We're not made of money, little birds.

EL PRECIO DE UN TAMAL

*And Mary Lou Perez said they took her mom into the
Emergency on Wednesday. She's been in a Home since she had
that stroke…*

*Ay, I'll light a candle for her. Mary Lou's mom was always so
nice at bingo.*

Boil the meat. Boil the chiles. Don't forget to season.
Soften the corn husks in water. Pick out los feos.

Did you hear about Dolores' son? His wife just left him.

No! Didn't he marry a Valdez?

*Si si, he married Tony's daughter. Well, Carmen was over there
visiting with Dolores and she said the wife pulled up
dumping all his clothes y todo at her house!*

Drain the meat. Save the stock. Melt the lard. Blend the chiles
up in the ugly blender, not the good one. Some for the meat.
Some for the masa. Mix the masa good. Get in there, not too
dry, not too salty.

*Lala's daughter just started school up North.
Lala said they dropped her off last week.*

She was always a good little girl. Nothing like
Lala at that age…You remember?

Spread the masa on the husk. Spoon in some meat. Put an olive.
No, no olives in this order. Line the tamales in the black pot.
Make sure the bottom has enough water to steam.

Spread the masa, chismoleras. Keep our stories tucked away for the next order.
Price of a good tamal is good chisme.

SOUNDS OF MY NEIGHBORHOOD

These are the sounds of my neighborhood:
The low mouth roar of passing cars,
smooth lowrider rumbles,
guttural troca thrums,
wailing sirens that bring brief pause.
Only brief,
and then the tinkling of paletero bells,
a cacophony of birds hung low on telephone
wires, bursts of music riding sonido waves.

Y tu te vas…

Vivo de tres animales…

…then it's the bomb, the bomb, the bomb…

The ticker tape click of tweaker bikes,
everywhere the weaving of words.

Hey Mando! What's up foo? How you been?

Sacate eso de la boca, Angel!

Mami!? I can't find my shoes!

If you can't find them, we're gonna leave you!

Laughter uninhibited in its own space,
the cackling glee,
the disbelieving snort,
Dude, shut the hell up. You're hella stupid!

The howling of the train,
joined by a chorus of backyard dogs.
Somewhere a sharp,
¡Cállate, Cookie!

A crescendo of crashing screen doors,
white noise whirl of plug-in fans,
gentle tones of young couples
passing the time,
hoses spouting water on thirsty plants
in the cool of evening.
Only in the evening
when the sun don't beat down.

These are the sounds of my neighborhood.

AMAYA ALEGRIA

Amaya calls it joy
with a fresh nail set
clicking in the Steinbeck Sun.
But she don't know him
cause her people don't buy grapes.
Alegria.
Cruising with her homegirls
through Mother's green hair tendrils,
faces kissed cool
as they cackle and curse
into a Northern breeze.
Alegria.
Amaya calls it joy
to paper her walls in drawings
drawn on prison envelopes
of roses not yet grown.
Gardens of her brother's design.
She calls it all
Alegria.

LAVENDER BUBBLES

Lavender colored bubbles
from Fabuloso flowers
leave my Tía Cuca's
linoleum floor
streaked clean.
Pásale, mija.
I step
into her perfumed home,
flowers and tortillas de maíz,
of ornate carpets,
plastic covered lace tablecloths,
and every cousins' wedding picture.
Pásale, mi chulita. Preciosa. ¿Cómo están?
I place a kiss
on her powder soft cheek.
There it is again.

LESSONS IN BEING A CHICANO MAN

I took my lessons in being a Chicano man behind my brothers,
following the discarded path in their rites of passage.

A Chicano man needs songs of love to feel,
homemade frijoles to eat,
shirts to iron out clean,
sainted mothers to hold up.

Cars to wash by hand,
shoes to keep from creasing,
and a faithful lady to dedicate all of these to.

Mostly, a Chicano man needs to see himself
in the eyes of his children,
in a tattoo of his name,

and in movies
made in his image.

Movies made in shorthand,
teatro with the dust shaken off.

Corny-lined Shakespeareans of the barrio
are where my brothers first see themselves.

American Me, a tragedy,
spoken in verse by that old maestro.

Blood In
my brother looks like Miklo.

Blood Out
my brother uses like Cruz.

My first crush wasn't Benny the Jet.
It was El Gallo Negro.

Lessons for my brothers to be
and for me just to see.

Poor Ritchie,
always a mother left to cry.

Poor Selena,
she had to deal with Chicano men too.

My brothers saw themselves
and crowed out gritos.

I saw them
and kept searching.

Elodia Esperanza Benitez

EVA WITH THE BIG MOUTH

Watch out
for
Eva with the Big Mouth.
Never knew a word
she wouldn't spit.
Eva with the loud voice
she wants
you to hear.
Forever ready to fight,
so says the Tía
caught spreading chismes.
So says the brother
throwing back opinions
like watery drinks.
So says the girl
staring too long.
Like, what
are you staring at?
Watch out
for
Eva with the Big Mouth.
Thinks she's all that.
Call her what you want,
don't matter to her.

ANTONIA DOESN'T WANT

ANYMORE BABIES

Antonia doesn't want anymore babies.
She didn't want the first, truth be told.
But her Mami was scandalized.
But her sister was excited.
But her boyfriend, Julio,
promised he'd be there.
And when she was lying there
burning in the aftermath,
Baby Girl on her chest
crying and splotchy colored,
she felt it all at once.
And when they sent her home
with Baby Girl and without Julio,
she felt very little.
Antonia remembered going out to dance bachata
whenever she wanted.
She remembered the thickness of her hair,
the smooth plane of her stomach,
when her vanity had bones to stand on.
She kissed and blamed her daughter.
She would warn her when the time came.
Julio came back and sure enough,
he wanted another baby to go with the first,
but Antonia doesn't want anymore babies.

TERRIBLE

The women in my family
are terribly beautiful.
Terrible like scorpion stings,
flowers that bloom by cracking cactus heads.
All of them
daughters of Narcissus and his melancholic disdain.
They are the ruination of lesser men,
features carved over centuries,
centered on bold brown noses,
smoldering beneath ruins with mouths
that cut with obsidian blades.
They are reconquistadoras,
takers of what you said they can't have.
Terrible like earthquakes that shake foundations,
the stirring perfume that guides us from our sleep.
The women in my family are
a terrible thing to behold.

THE BALLAD OF IMELDA ALEJO

VILLA: PART TWO

Ayer ya paso, Dios mío
He came in the night.
He came like a thief in the night,
that faceless man.
Cowards have no faces.

Mañana, quizá no vendrá
Lurking in the dark between floodlights,
he saw her.
He saw Imelda standing out amongst the rose bushes.
Drunk with the anger of entitled men,
he took his gun
and shot her down.

Ayúdame hoy
He didn't see her fall
out amongst the rose bushes,
he didn't hear her children cry out,
didn't know they saw.

Yo quiero vivir un día la vez
Suffer the little children.
Bring them to their mother.
But she was shot down
taken by the jealousy
of another.

LA BALADA DE IMELDA ALEJO

VILLA: SEGUNDA PARTE

Ayer ya pasó, Dios mío
El vino en la noche.
Vino como un ladrón en la noche,
ese hombre sin rostro.
Los cobardes no tienen cara.

Mañana, quizá no vendrá
Acechando en la oscuridad entre reflectores,
el la vio a ella.
Vio a Imelda de pie entre los rosales.
Borracho con la ira de los hombres con derecho
tomó su arma
y le disparó.

Ayúdame hoy
No la vio caer
entre los rosales.
No escuchó a sus hijos gritar.
No sabía que vieron.

Yo quiero vivir un día a la vez
Dejen que los niños vengan.
Llévalos a su madre,
pero ella fue derribada.
Tomada por los celos
de otro.

PARTING WORDS

Parting words to the girl that I was
as the last vestiges of you
fade from my face.
I smiled today,
laughed loud enough to turn heads,
let the sun redden my bare shoulder,
blasted my music.
I did it in joy.
You have known
too many days
that allowed little joy.
Now, I bask in it.
Oh, girl.
How loved I am now
with friends who call
to ask the time of day.
Family close to heart.
No need to fight
for my measure of peace anymore.
The words have never left,
my constant companions.
We do our dance.
No need to worry for me,
my girl.
Fade away and let me be new.

I HAVE NO HEROES

I am seventeen when it goes bad,
worse than what it was.
And what it was
was sleeping couch side with biting spiders,
answering the door tweaker fathers
coming to ask for two dollars.
Ma choosing between groceries or rent or PG&E.
Big back, floor sitting TV,
no cable, just Channel Two news and *That 70's Show.*
At seventeen
my brother Isaiah gets arrested.
No money for lawyers,
no sympathy for nineteen year old thieves,
twenty years to grind the maíz out of him.
Ma won't get out of bed, it's happened before,
I know what to do.
I can get a job, make the dinners,
wash the clothes, walk the kids to school.
Nana gets sick.
By the time we find out,
she's floating and fading away.
She dies waiting for the priest
the day a letter from Isaiah arrives
telling her to get well soon.

The floor breaks beneath my feet.
I get the mail to see that our street
is being rechristened Cesar Chavez Avenue.
Boulevards, avenues,
libraries, and parks for our fabled heroes.
I have no heroes.
Cesar didn't walk for me.
Dolores doesn't know my name.
Pancho didn't ride out to free me.
Emiliano has no words for people already on their knees.
I must do what I always do,
I must be my own hero.

PERILS OF A PRETTY MOM

She leaves a maroon kiss mark
on her daughter's cheek
before she leaves for work.
Try to catch her,
perilous to be so pretty.
Who could she be?
Were it not for…
Perils of a pretty mom.
Isn't she feather haired and lovely?
Eyes like lightning struck wood —
earth in some parts,
burnt in some parts —
high ridge cheekbones,
tattoo her name in ink,
dedicate a song to her teartracks,
paint her into Itza.

CALLADITAS

Belinda Beltran never has much to say.
Muy calladita
at school, at work, at parties with loud primas
already using up the words.
Will her own words come out right?
The way she thinks them?
Muy calladita,
they say of her,
to slip by unseen.
Belinda knows it's easier to watch
if they don't know you're watching.
If they don't see, if they don't hear you.

VIEWS FROM THE NUMBER 68

Views from the Number 68 bus
caught along Monterey
where I stood waiting
on the edge of tomorrow and yesterday
yearning to leave the land of technology
for the farm rows thirty minutes south.
Next to me,
a man in a bent SF ball cap,
backpack hefted heavy on his shoulders.
Paying me no mind, headphones in his ears.
The number 68 roars into sight.
Smells of exhaust and tire rubber,
rattles and shudders as it rolls,
lurches forward to sigh.
Bus driver nodding us on with a sigh and wave
when ballcap man doesn't have enough change.
Always thank your bus driver.
Views from the Number 68 bus
packed with folks
going the same direction.
Bleary eyed winos dozing,
fast food workers with hair pulled back tight,
students tapping at phones,
sun weary seniors with well used walkers.

Views from the Number 68 bus,
the land finally starts to taper flat.
Breathing room between buildings,
grassy yellowed hills to the back,
pot-holed roads,
liquor stores flick by.
The sudden swoop to a stop
next to St.Mary's Church.
Lapsed Catholic that I am,
throw a quick *Sign of the Cross*.
Someone grabs a bike with bag of cans tied to the back.
Rattle, rattle, rattle.
Last view of the Number 68 bus
pulling into a pink stone station.

PRISCILLA HAS AN UNCLE

Priscilla has an uncle.

Priscilla has an uncle she loves very much.

Priscilla has an uncle she loves very much,
who drinks too much.

Priscilla has an uncle she loves very much,
who drinks too much, but never gets mean.

Priscilla has an uncle she loves very much,
who drinks too much, but never gets mean,
he's just sad.

I SAW YOUR TATA TODAY

I saw your Tata today,
He's the viejito who walks with his little cart,
right? Envelope of scratchers in his pocket,
A's cap on his head,
list in his hand for milk and bread.
I offered him a ride but he said no,
He couldn't leave his cart.
I saw your Tata again today
with his basket of laundry
taking his time.
He said he likes to get out of the house,
now and again.

CITLALI OF MANY FACES

Citlali Fuentes wears many faces.
Chin up scowls
for folks with staring problems.
Eyes rolled right
for principals on power trips.
Stoic stare
for cops who stop her cold,
good for all types.
Citlali keeps her faces
in her back pocket.
A set for home too.
Smile Now face,
for her sister's sake,
softest one she keeps.
Raised up brows
for mom's accusations.
Laughing face with teeth flashed
for her dumbass friends.
Closest to her own,
a little goofy,
tired and off kilter,
that one she saves,
keeps it just for her.

WOMEN IN THE RAIN

Trauma taught lessons
I hadn't meant to retain,
kept me sitting atop my apartment stairs
mapping constellations in the night sky,
grief had not given names.
Staring out my window into my neighborhood,
which may as well have been,
the world in its entirety.
I watched from my window,
watched the women dancing,
laughing as they went about their weaving.
Their songs climbing up my apartment stairs
as they laid down flowers.
I, alone, watched from my window.
I heard the drums before I heard the rain.
Saw from my window
the women dancing in the rain.
Standing, stomping,
moving to the thunder drum beat.
I, against my window,
couldn't stand in the rain with them.
I went out,
took the first step down my apartment stairs.

THE SONS AND DAUGHTERS OF IMELDA ALEJO VILLA: PART ONE

Tu ya viviste, entre los hombres
Suffer the little children,
now without a mother,
scattered to the winds,
by the act of another.

Tu sabes, mi Dios, que hoy esta peor
Two daughters,
still with milk teeth,
sent away on an East Wind.
One daughter sent to wander the West,
two sons sent North to work,
and the eldest son,
who refused to move from the spot
where his mother fell.

Es mucho dolor
For days
he lay amongst the nettle,
thorns seeping bitter into his heart.
And when the eldest son moved,
it was for revenge.
Moving openly
in the glare of flood lights,
he found the faceless man.

Hay mucho egoísmo
y mucha maldad
Señor, por mi bien
Yo quiero vivir, un día la vez

LOS HIJOS E HIJAS DE IMELDA

ALEJO VILLA: PRIMERA PARTE

Tú ya viviste entre los hombres
Dejen que los niños vengan
ahora sin madre,
dispersos a los vientos
por el acto de otro.

Tú sabes, mi Dios, que hoy está peor
Dos hijas, todavía con dientes de leche
enviadas lejos con el viento del este.
Una hija, enviada a vagar por el oeste,
dos hijos, enviados al norte a trabajar.
Y el hijo mayor
quien se negó a moverse del lugar
donde se cayó su madre.

Es mucho dolor
Por muchos días, acostado entre ortigas,
espinas amargas filtran su corazón.
Y cuando el hijo mayor se movió
fue por venganza.
Moviéndose libremente
en el resplandor de los reflectores,
encontró al hombre sin rostro.

Hay mucho egoísmo
y mucha maldad
Señor, por mi bien
yo quiero vivir, un día la vez

STILL ELENA

Elena looked in the mirror one morning,
strong of leg, strong of arm,
not so strong of back.
Realized the color was fading from her hair.
Still pretty in braids, still pretty in flowers,
still canela colored in some places.
Work had weathered her hands,
made the bones of her feet crack.
This morning, Strong Elena
with another twenty years to go,
color starting to fade from her hair,
still Elena.

VISIONS OF A WOMAN IN SUCCESS

Visions of a woman in success:
District Attorney of Santa Clara County
in a skirt suit
carrying a buckle snap briefcase
stands near Letty.
Close enough to see
Letty in her baby face of fourteen
dressed in her mother's cardigan for court.
Family clucked together in their yearning fear,
but District Attorney can't see
her eyes having been plucked out
for blind justice's sake.
Letty can see,
can see how District Attorney,
Judge,
Public Defender,
all act out the tragedy
in well-known roles.
Can see how they laugh
about weekends spent under a gentler sun,
sees how casually they run for time.
Her brother has to go to prison
for taking what wasn't his,
but he's on their stage now.

District Attorney has never seen
a child's face
on a brown boy.
To her, they spring from Earth,
with faces hard as flint,
harsh dialects from snake mouths.
Brown boys need
to be sent back to ground before they bite.
Letty wants to leap forward,
with a wail of *Please.*
His name is Ramon.
Mama used to call him monito
when he was little.
So, you see? He was a child once.
But as soon as she opens her mouth,
they pull off their ears, and close the curtain.

SEVEN GENERATIONS

I've got seven generations
of grief stunted ambitions sitting on me.

No offense toward any daughters of mine.
But you are not the sum total
of my hopes and dreams.
Allow me to shake a few of these off
by way of trips to Myrtle Beach
and other places void of Spanish saint names.

Let me carve my own Spanish name
into a few places, Daughter.

So I don't pass my load onto you.

YADIRA, YESSICA, YOLANDA, YESENIA, YARITZY

Yadira, Yessica, Yolanda, Yesenia, Yaritzy,
walk the mile.
A line of five far back on the track,
sweatpants in late summer,
on a cement dust track ruining their Vans,
strolling slower every time PE coach yells
for them to hustle.
Talking real good shit today.
Yaritzy is going to fight Marisa after school
for trying to message her boyfriend
underneath a mural painted by
college educated Chicano art students
so caught up in their first generation fervor
they painted themselves
into the faces of the farmworkers and the grapes.
It ain't over a guy, it's 'cause she disrespected me.
Four nods in agreement.
Yesenia is often accused of disrespect
by office administrators
sitting in portable buildings,
where footsteps thud hollow.
They don't scare her.

At home, accusations of disrespect,
come close to the face,
You think you're all big and bad now, huh?
Yolanda wonders if the President's Fitness Test
takes into account all the brown girls
who slow walk the mile in protest
of being told when to run.
As if they haven't been running
every minute of every day.
Yessica wonders when she gets to rest.
Maybe, when she graduates?
Maybe, when she validates
seven generations of hard work?
You are what your parents dreamed of
when they came to this country.
Yessica wonders whose parents they mean,
because hers came over to afford a roof
for the house they're building in Rosarito.
The dream sold to Dreamers
isn't one she's ever bought.
Yadira doesn't dream of tomorrow.
All she's ever heard from sun-lined abuelos,
and dads staying in halfway houses,

Tomorrow isn't promised, mija.
It's truer than any word
from her school counselor
who promises tomorrow at the expense of today.
Yadira knows there's no tomorrow.
No tomorrow for her brother locked up.
No tomorrow for her friend shot at a party.
She's guaranteed this mile today.
Walking the track with her homegirls,
Yadira, Yessica, Yolanda, Yesenia, Yaritzy
finish their lap.

SHE REDUCES ME

My Mama reduces me
into a little girl
with a painful lump
in my throat.
A very childish pain
at the thought of being without her.
Reduces me
to the softest part of myself.
A well-earned weakness,
by virtue of her love.
Let her never be out of my reach.
My Mama reduces me into
the parts of myself she created.

GOOD JOB

Rosanna leaves for work in the dark of morning
floating between tired and wired from routine.

It's a —
good job, good benefits,
good job, good benefits.

The 101 is a four lane open stretch
all the way to San Jose.
She passes towering titans
with tent city campfires in their shadows.

For that —
good job, good benefits,
good job, good benefits.

Rosanna's been clocking in
for twenty six years at her job
since her oldest was in diapers.

She needed —
good job, good benefits,
good job, good benefits.

The work creaks the back,
the work cricks the neck,
leaves the hands cracked.
What are you gonna do?

It's a —
good job, good benefits,
good job, good benefits.

Her oldest won't work for the job,
a daughter talking in fantasies.
She doesn't want to live for

only a —
good job, good benefits,
good job, good benefits.

Rosanna wonders when
she forgot to teach necessity of work,
of doing what you have to do,
supporting yourself, head held high.

All for —
good job, good benefits,
good job, good benefits.

Rosanna's daughter has watched her mom
come home tired for twenty-six years.

ALONDRA, CALLED DOLORES

For Juliana and Na'el Benitez

Alondra has a little hummingbird
fluttering away inside of her.
And before soft wing beats gain strength
for others to marvel at,
she'll keep these moments to herself.
She writes out a list
of all the names that mean Joy.

But sometimes, little birds...

Alondra wakes silent
and still.
It seems her little hummingbird
has flown away in the night.
Alondra renames herself Dolores.
She writes out
all the names that mean Sorrow
for the stillness inside.

She goes all winter
without seeing any birds,
which is just as well.
It's much too cold where she is.

But then…

Spring brings a kinder sun,
blooms of blue forget-me-nots,
the clipper buzz of bees,
warm sprinkles of rain.
Alondra, called Dolores,
begins to look for new names
for a new season.
And finally…finally
she feels the flutter of wings.

RUINS

Rachel Romana lies in ruins
left somewhere to bake in the sun off
Pacheco Pass, or winding down Hecker Pass
with clusters of field workers
picking fruit from white columns.
Rachel Romana first learned to read
by passing produce signs selling strawberries.
This place within breadth of the ocean
is out of reach by endless lines of green
needing to be picked first.
She touches the land.
When Rachel Romana brought her daughter
into her world of flat valley farmland,
she named her Reina Romana.
Promised she would always live here.

NAME HER ESPERANZA

For Sophia Dolores Esperanza Jaramillo

Name her Esperanza,
not for hope's sake.
Give her a name
to yell when she isn't listening,
to curl and prick like bush thorns.

Name her Esperanza,
it makes for big tattoos,
wants for softness,
but falls too bold off the tongue.

Name her Esperanza,
let her rumble through it.
She'll unsettle bones
like passing thunder,
long enough to grow into,
settle her spine into.

Name her Esperanza,
not for hope,
but for what it takes.

OLDEST DAUGHTER

I am an oldest daughter, born to my role.
I am my mother's emotional soundboard.
I am my father's server of plates.
I am second mother to my brother.
I am made up of all the things I am to others,
tethered by a well hewn sense of responsibility,
tethered by love, and the notion that no one else
can do what I do.
Twisted up with the unfinished laundry
is my resentment
washed away by guilt
when I see my brother's face.
Feelings of maternity meet
with sibling squabbles.
The hand that pinches
is the hand that soothes scraped knees.
I am older than my own face.
I am the oldest daughter.

ON RONAN STREET

Gravel dirt goes poorly with freshly cleaned Corteses.
But I walked everywhere in those days,
full regalia.
We lived on Ronan Street.
A little ways from the action, from the park,
from the kickbacks,
though in those days
the action would come to us.
Come to the front door of my Tía's house
asking for my prima and I,
quick with a joke,
quick with something to smoke.
My prima and I held court for jesters in Dickies
trying to make us laugh.
I, a guest in my Tía's house,
one of many, like the last Tía's house.
Cruising with the homegirls,
smoke curling around the turn from Ronan onto Monterey.
I dressed cleaner than the dudes in those days,
always ironed, always feathered, always ready.
Who wants to be in the house?
Shared stuffy rooms with stoves forever boiling,
noticias between novelas.
Wasn't me.

Maybe homebodies have more peace.
I always knew I would have to work hard for mine.
Girls who wear burgundy lip liner know the ways of the world.
I was magnificent then, Linda Gloriana,
in those Ronan Street days.

SEMILLAS FOR GILAS

Michael's mother plants roses all over East 8th Street.
Roses planted in dedication
to those in front St. Mary's,
where her mother knelt beside her father
exchanging vows
in the days before he shipped out to Vietnam.
She stands outside in the cool of evening,
water hose in hand, sprinkling seeds.

Scatter the seeds.
Semillas we leave behind,
water them to grow
into tomorrow's garden.

Michael's father heads off to work
before dawn touches the valley hills.
His truck ambling through downtown,
Old Monterey taking him through
Old Charrito, sitting sideline with viejo rights.
He places his hand out the window
to sprinkle seeds along the streets.

Scatter the seeds.
Semillas we leave behind,
water them to grow
into tomorrow's garden.

Michael rides his bike
from the spot where Las Animas was razed,
down past the levy
where they raised it back up,
collecting his friends as he goes.
They fly past vendors selling flowers and fruit,
fruit grown in fields close to home,
the very same his great grandfather once bent to harvest.
Boys on bikes picking up seeds in their wheels
depositing them everywhere they go.

Scatter the seeds.
Semillas we leave behind,
water them to grow
into tomorrow's garden.

When Michael was little,
like many before him,
he was taken to Chitactac
to be shown holes worn into rock,
and asked if he could hear the Ohlone
calling up from the shallow bottoms.

SUNDAY NIGHT OLDIES SHOUTOUTS

I'd like to dedicate a song to Ruben Alvarez. We been together seven years and I just wanna say that I'll always love you, baby. And when you get out, I'll be here.

Uh, can you play a song for my mom? She passed away five years ago today and she loved her oldies. It ain't the same without her... I love you, Mama!

I just broke up with my girlfriend. We were together for six years and I'm really going through it right now. Can you play me something?

I wanna give a shoutout to Moni Rios. I love you and I'm sorry for everything I put you through. I'm going to be the man you need me to be.

Can you play a song for me and my daughter? Her name is Janessa and she's the biggest blessing in my life.

CRUISING ON A MEMORY

Primo Hermano, this evening I took a cruise for you. The day
was hot in that searing way, in that bounces back on the
black top way. The evening though, was cool
in that wonderful South Bay way, in that Northern breeze
brushing across the face way. Sunday evenings are for
Brenton Wood and Mary Wells, for Sam Cooke
and Ritchie Valens,
for "Suavecito" played on repeat. People make a lot
of things that change when you're gone. And sure, maybe,
the old Pinocchio's Pizza is closed,
maybe they built an Amazon warehouse on our farmland,
maybe they finally demolished the old junior high school,
maybe a new family lives in Nana's house on Polk Ct.
But, time doesn't move as swiftly as you might think
and the park bench at Miller Park,
where you had your tenth birthday, is still there. I cruised
past all of it like the Sentinel of Memory that I am for you.
There will come a time, when we're both two old heads
reminiscing at the carne asada
in the chairs our grandkids set out for us,
when everything will be very different. For now,
Primo Hermano, I promise you,
not everything is as different as you might think.

VEINTENA

For Yolanda Teotleyaocihuatl Castro

Beats that thud the chest
so as to reset the heart rhythm,
vibrating through the auditorium in visible vapor air.
Rattling the wooden pews,
shaking loose what I had thought concrete.
Brown feet in old step,
stomach hollowed out with the drum.
I don't know the steps,
but the beat is familiar.
Spinning colors
rushing at each other,
calls cutting through
spiking the blood.
I am more alive in this moment
than all my moments before.
Babies learning the steps,
little girl matching with stilted steps,
a woman arches with bird grace,
flowers at her feet, flowers at the feet of the drums.
Dip, dip, dip.
Sweat off her brow, sweat off her back,
slower now, but relentless.

Tap and cross,
and turn and stomp.
A shell horn blows.
I am no longer spectating.
My heart rushes forward as they do,
thudding all the time
with the drum.

THE EXCHANGE

Pati will end up with her parents. She's known it
since she bought a home of her own and filled it
with painted clay bowls instead of babies.
Her sisters are married. Her brothers
have a gang of babies already. Some of them
look a bit like Pati. It's enough to be Tía to them
and Mama to the chiles growing in her garden.
She has time after work making her own dinner
to answer her mom's calls. She has time
to pick her dad up on Saturday mornings
for the pulga on Berryessa. Pati exchanged wedding vows
with her freedom long ago. She cultivates time in her garden,
gives it back as rides to doctor appointments,
and the grocery store. She stops by twice a week for dinner,
and makes sure their pills are in order. In a few days,
Pati will call up one of her sisters or maybe one of her brothers,
harp at them about helping out more. But,
daughters on their own, always give it back somehow.

THE SONS AND DAUGHTERS OF IMELDA

ALEJO VILLA: FINALE

Ayer ya paso, Dios mío
Mañana, quizás no vendra
There came a day,
many days
after Imelda had been dedicated to the Earth.
A daughter sent to wander West
turned South for home,
two daughters sent East
turned their heads,
two sons in the North
looked up from their work.

Ayúdame, hoy
A wandering daughter
had seen all the West had to offer,
had slept under many roofs,
but called no one mother.
Two daughters sent East
had been given new names,
could scarcely remember their first.
Two sons working in the North
had put their memories away tight,
and yet some persist
like the combing prayers
of beautiful callused hands.

Yo quiero vivir
Suffer the little children.
Bring them to their mother,
but she was shot down
taken by the jealousy
of another.

Un día a la vez
The sons and daughters,
of Imelda Alejo Villa
scattered to the winds,
walked up the hillside
together,
found a field of rose bushes,
and their eldest brother waiting.

LOS HIJOS E HIJAS DE IMELDA

ALEJO VILLA: FINAL

Ayer ya pasó, Dios mío
Mañana, quizás no vendrá
Llegó un día,
muchos días
después de que Imelda fue enterrada a la tierra.
Una hija vagando por el oeste
giró al sur hacia su hogar.
Dos hijas que fueron enviadas al este
voltieron sus rostros.
Dos hijos en el norte
levantaron sus cabezas de su trabajo.

Ayúdame, hoy
Una hija errante
vio todo lo que el oeste tenía para ofrecer.
Dormio bajo muchos techos
pero no llamó a nadie madre.
Dos hijas enviadas al este
tenían nuevos nombres
y apenas podían recordar la primera.
Dos hijos trabajando en el norte
guardaron sus memorias pero,
sin embargo, algunas persisten.
Como las oraciones peinadas
con manos hermosas y callosas.

Yo quiero vivir
Dejen que los niños vengan.
Llévalos a su madre,
pero ella fue derribada.
Tomada por los celos
de otro.

Un día a la vez
los hijos e hijas
de Imelda Alejo Villa,
dispersos a los vientos,
caminaron juntos bajando la ladera.
Encontraron un campo de rosales
y su hermano mayor esperando.

Elodia Esperanza Benitez

WE SIT GRAVESIDE

My Nana took me by the hand,
plastic dollar store flowers in other hand
to sit graveside at the spot
where her own Nana Julia had been buried.
She let me push the hard stems into the damp cemetery mud,
pretty flowers seeming to burst from the ground,
surrounding a fading picture set in headstone.
We sat graveside.
My Nana planted memories
deep enough in the mud that I
could see her Nana Julia,
despite the fading picture,
standing white gloved at the foot of St. Mary's steps,
open-armed to welcome my Nana, a little girl,
into her embrace.
Recognized the words of love
as those my Nana spoke over me.
We sit graveside
with flowers bursting from my chest.
Nanas live forever in the love and words they plant within us.
I sit graveside, gardening my memories.

ACKNOWLEDGMENTS

I want to thank my mother Herlinda. Ma, for as long as I can remember you were waking up before the sun to go to work, or coming home from a graveyard shift. You have always been beautiful and strong and genuinely giving. Our living room can attest to the number of folks you let stay with us when they fell on hard times. You never draw attention to the good that you do for others. It was you who encouraged my love of reading, who brought me back boxes of yard sale books. It was you who showed me the true meaning of perseverance, going after your career as a transit mechanic and taking care of Ysidro and me by yourself. If I haven't said it, I say now that I admire you. You and I have learned how to be mother and daughter together. We have cultivated our bond and it's the most cherished one in my life.

I want to thank my brother Ysidro, whom I love most in this world. Brother Bear, I have been so very blessed in this life to be your sister. It's almost difficult to put it into words. You make me laugh and you get on my nerves. You know me better than anyone else but you always seem to surprise me. You're the only person I can sit in complete silence with. You move through life quietly and constant, a necessary calm. I am overwhelmed by how proud I am of the man you've become, of how proud Nana would be. I want all the happiness and good things of this world for you, Ysidro.

I want to thank my family for all their love and support.

Brenda, my beautiful aunt full of dreams and talent, you have always encouraged me. As a kid, I loved to watch you style your hair and put on makeup or to ride with you up to Richmond, soft rock hits and cumbias playing all the way up there. I wanted to be just like you.

Amaya, you wonderful and crazy kid. God sent you down just to raise my blood pressure. You are braver and bolder than people twice your age. You are fearless and motivated. You inspire me and you make my life brighter simply by existing. I don't just love you, kid…I adore you.

Angel Lara, you're my uncle and I love you.

Neena, my best friend and sister. You saved me from myself. I was never young until the first time you made me laugh so hard I screamed. I was so sad before you busted into my life through the office door at South Valley Middle School. For the past fifteen years, you have been my rock. What would I have done without you? Who would I be? We have been through just about everything and carried each other through it. To quote your favorite show, "You're my person." More than that, you're my other half.

Jacob, cousin, there is a day somewhere in the near future where we are both sitting at a table laughing and cracking jokes, probably eating some bomb food made by myself. You have been strong for everyone, for me. The long road you've been traveling on is about to go somewhere beautiful with that beautiful baby girl you have. Na'el is and always will be the greatest gift to come out of this time in our lives. You, Ysidro, and I know what it was like in that old house on Polk Ct. We carry Nana with us everywhere we go, those prayers she spoke over us are alive and coming true today. Soon, cousin, soon we'll be at that table.

To my maddening Aunt Lisa and cousin Shudie (Ernesto), you guys are physically far but never far from my heart. Our visits together are some of my favorite moments and memories. Lisa, the constant traveller, who brings us out of our comfort zone and challenges us to imagine a world bigger than where we call home. Shudie, you're going to reach places academically and professionally that a lot of us never came close to. You've become a good young man, a rarity and a credit to your parents. I love you both, I love Neto, all of my family over there in Wisconsin, and of course, Ricky.

My Uncle Gelacio, Aunt Ana, Rachel, Angie, Sarah, and Oliver; I'll keep you together because when I think of what a family should be, I think of you all. Ana and Gelacio, the family you've built is made up of baseball and dancing, art and day trips around the Bay, safety and unconditional love. It's beautiful.

My Uncle Cayetano, Aunt Anngiela, JC, Joseph, Aleignna, Dalisay, and Anne — I'll be visiting my vacation home real soon. I love you all to pieces. Cayetano and Anghie, you've created a home full of noise and joy, it's one of my favorite places to be. To my cousins, you're so dear and wonderful to me. Dalisay and Anne, we will forever be blessed that when my awesome aunt joined our family, you did as well.

Para mi Grandpa Leandro, te quiero mucho.
Sabrina, you do a lot for the people you love. I am a living example. You have fed me, clothed me, both dropped off and picked me up from school, listened to my rants, supported my interests, showed me some top tier music, and let me sit passenger side to some lovely car rides. Your humor, your quick fire wit, your unmatchable self is deserving of recognition. You have been there for me again and again. You deserve your flowers.

Aunt Jenny, Uncle Camilo, Angel, Marcos, Carlos, Lilly, my Nino Camilo, my Nina Angie, Lala and Michael, the De La Cuevas. I would not be where I am without your love and support. Ysidro and I have never gone through hardships alone with you all beside us. So many of my happiest memories have your faces shining through.

I want to acknowledge the wonderful community of artists and friends in my life. Rosanna Alvarez, who I first met as a twelve year old girl. Who would have thought we would be here today? You encouraged me and spoke a permission I didn't know I needed to hear to give life to the poetry I kept sleeping in my notebook pages. Armando Franco, my fellow Vato Loco for Life, my dear friend who reminds us that Gilroy has always had breadth and color. The cover you created for this collection was more than I imagined. Wonderful, crazy, dedicated Lizette Diaz: you motivate me to never stop pursuing my passions and to work tirelessly for my community and loved ones. You are the definition of self-made. I am lucky to call you my friend. Yolanda Teotleyaocihuatl Castro, you are an inspiration. You have taught me what it truly means to have palabra, to honor and celebrate culture, to work within and for the community.
I also want to acknowledge EASTSIDE Magazine, a publication out of Eastside San Jose and one of the first to feature my work.

A thank you to the teachers and staff at Mt. Madonna Continuation High School, without whom I may not have graduated at all. Mrs. Del Bono, Ms. Gonzalez, Mrs. Cohen, Mr. Ward, Mr.Gemar, and Mr. Charvet…you made all the difference at that time in my life.

And to my loved ones who have since passed on into the next life. You were with me throughout this process. To my Big Nana Manuela, Big Tata Emilio, Tía Nati, Aunt Pila, Aunt Sarah, Tío Ramon, and my niece Juliana Faith.

ABOUT THE ARTIST

Armando Franco is a Chicano/Mexican-American visual & public artist based in the South Bay Area and Central Coast of California. After receiving his Bachelor's of Art degree at California State University at Monterey Bay, Armando helped complete multiple mural restoration projects of Historic Chicano murals in his hometown of Gilroy, CA. Armando has collaborated with numerous community-based organizations and was also included in the Califas Legacy Project: The Ancestral Journey with the Monterey Museum of Art. Today, Armando's studio is located at 6th St. Studios and Art Center (Gilroy) and continues to work within the tri-county area. He is also currently a member of the Gilroy Arts Roundtable, which is a newly formed artist collective focused on developing a thriving arts community in Gilroy. You can find him on Instagram @adfranco_art

ABOUT THE AUTHOR

Elodia Esperanza Benitez is a Mexican American poet from Gilroy, CA bringing the strength of her ancestors and heritage to her work. She began writing at an early age as a way of processing her experiences and those around her. Her poems bring to life those closest to her by way of inviting their voices to sweep across the page. You can find her work in EASTSIDE magazine, the MALCS  (Mujeres Activas en Letras y Cambio Social) journal, and on her Instagram page @elodiabenitez.

ABOUT THE PUBLISHER

Riot of Roses Publishing House was founded in 2021 specifically to amplify the stories of historically silenced voices.

Xicana owned. Mujerista focused. For the people.

We publish books that heal and liberate.

Read our rebellion.

www.riotofrosespublishinghouse.com

RIOT OF ROSES
PUBLISHING HOUSE
SEJATNGA
UNCEDED TONGVA TERRITORY
SOUTH WHITTIER, CALIFORNIA